Snowmen are not all the same.
Most of them are pretty tame.

But Stevie, he was quite the hoot, for Stevie really loved to toot.

Now, snowman toots are not like ours, although they still don't smell like flowers!
And yes, they make a big loud rasp, that make some people jump and gasp.

But they are also cold as ice,
if you catch that breeze, it's not so nice.
They shoot out frost, hailstones, and snow,
a blizzard from their butts sure does blow!

Now, Stevie lived in an igloo, with his parents, as you might do.
They didn't like for their son to toot. They thought it was rude and not too cute.

So when Stevie came of age, he went out to earn a wage.
To get himself out of this "toot-free-zone", so that he could poot in his own home.

The first job he managed to score was at the local superstore.
SPERMARKET
In the carpark, collecting carts, while dropping many chilly farts.

His toots were wet and filled with frost, thus his toots came with a cost.
Each time he pumped, though it felt nice, he glazed the carpark with black ice.

The cars they lost control and grip.
They'd swerve, and screech, and slide, and whip.

P
S PERMARKET
One truck even crashed into a tree!
Stevie thought, "Maybe this job's just not for me."

So Stevie tried his luck elsewhere, maybe he had a chef's cooking flair!
A fancy restaurant took him on, a big chef's hat did Stevie don.

Although Stevie could hold a pan,
and chop a sprout, or roast a ham,
his toots, they still got in the way,
causing chaos through the day!

Kitchens must always be hot,
but with his farts, they just were not.

Each chilly whiff stole every flame.
They could not cook; he was to blame!

And all the food, it went out cold.
The customers would always shout and scold!
So Stevie's boss did make it clear,
"Your tooting is not welcome here."

“Education? Now there’s a job for me!
I’ll start teaching geography.”
I know about maps, I sure am clever,
and I’ll teach them all about cold weather!”
Toot

But even though he had the brain,
his toots caused havoc once again.

HA HA
All the kids and half the staff,
could do nothing else but laugh!

Laughter drowned out Stevie's speech, thus nobody could ever hear him teach!
HA HA
Every job he'd tried was tough, and Stevie thought he'd had enough.

He walked the streets with his head down, not even one fart-friendly job in town.
To cheer himself, he tried a toot, one that was tuneful like a flute.

As usual, it came with ice and snow,
making it slippery down below.

WOOoHoo!!
Suddenly, a young fox whizzed past.
He was making noise and moving fast.

"I'm sorry!" Stevie said to him.
"I didn't mean to make you skim."
"Why not?" the fox laughed with a wink.
"It was as fun as an ice rink!"

"Ice rink, you say," the snowman mused.
"I know a field that is unused."
And to this field he promptly went,
with his ice rink making intent.

He tooted ice, put up a wall,
hung up some lights, more snow did fall.

What now stood was a rink of ice.
In order to rent it, he'd charge a price!

He opened "Stevie's Tooty Rink". And though it had a tooty stink,
STEVIE'S TOOTY RINK
The local kids would come on by, across the rink they all would fly.

At last Stevie had found a way,
to make his tooting habit pay.
STEVIE'S TOOTY RINK
STEVIE'S TOOTY RINK
STEVIE'S TOOTY RINK
So popular it became, he opened more.
He now owned "Tooty Rinks" galore!

The igloo that he bought was large,
a home in which he was in charge.
Parp
Toot
Pump
Guff
Pop
Bomp
Prrrrtt
He would toot there till the sun went down,
with no one there to boss 'em around.

Snowmen are not all the same.
Most of them are pretty tame.
But Stevie, he was quite the hoot,
for Stevie really loved to toot!

Made in the USA
Las Vegas, NV
22 November 2022

59869322R00021